Wonderful Hair

The Beauty of Annie Malone

By Eve Nadel Catarevas

Illustrated By Felicia Marshall

Creston Books

When Annie Malone started arranging her collection of combs, brushes, rollers, and mirrors on the kitchen table, everybody in the Turnbo house knew it was time to play beauty parlor.

Annie circled her older sister in silence. She was working on her hair plan.

Twist it?

Thread it?

Weave it?

Braid it?

Updo, down-do,

all-around-the-town-do?

You never knew what you were going to look like after time spent in Annie's chair. You just knew you'd look magnificent!

Even grown-ups wanted Annie's magic fingers in their hair. Annie's neighbor, Lillie, had a huge, tangled heap of hair. While fixing it up one day, Annie explained how she was going to learn everything she could about hair because hair was her destiny!

"Don't be silly," Lillie said. "Black girls like us grow up to be maids, washerwomen, or cooks."

"We'll see about that," Annie whispered.

As she got older, Annie noticed that many of her sisters' friends had patches of missing hair or blisters on their scalps caused by harsh hair straightening products. Or from the goose fat, bacon grease, or butter many used to tame rebellious curls and kinks. It made Annie sad. After all, they just wanted to look pretty.

Annie's aunt was an herb doctor, so Annie asked her if she could make something to help hair grow. Aunt Mary took a pinch from here, a dash from there. She mashed them together, added thick yellow liquid, and shook it all up. This formula would become the main ingredient in all of Annie's hair products. Annie insisted on paying. "One dime will do," Aunt Mary said. That purchase would change Annie Malone's life forever.

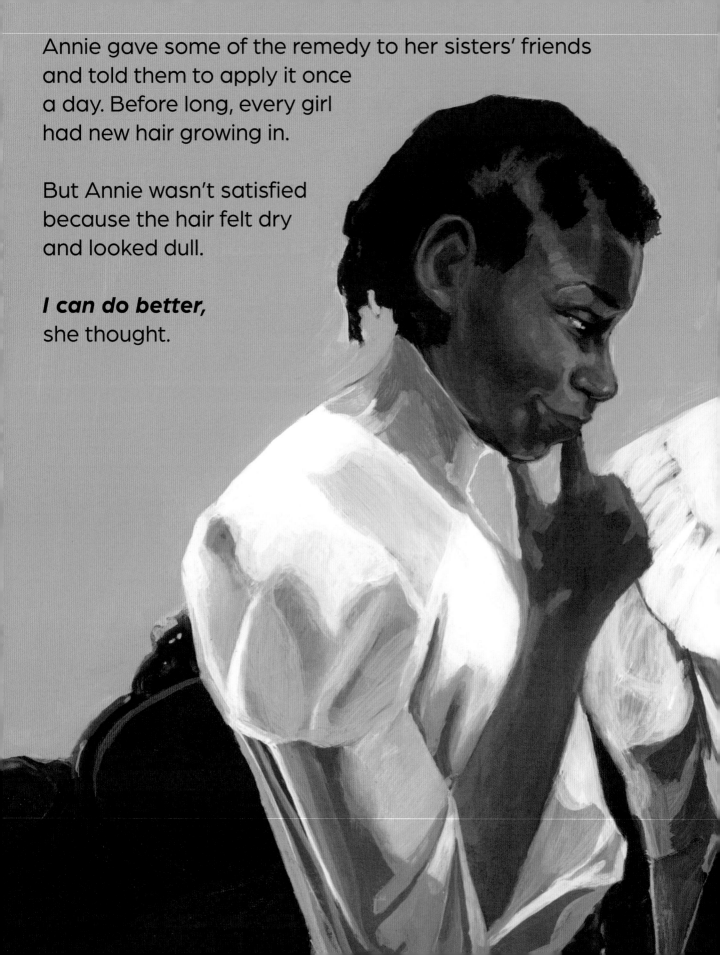

Annie gave some of the remedy to her sisters' friends and told them to apply it once a day. Before long, every girl had new hair growing in.

But Annie wasn't satisfied because the hair felt dry and looked dull.

I can do better, she thought.

Aunt Mary had taught Annie the power of herbs. Now she learned to use them herself, figuring out new combinations. Some worked well but smelled horrible. Others smelled nice but didn't work. Annie kept at it. One day, an ad for cow ointment in a farmer's manual caught her eye. Maybe the lotion could work on hair, too!

Annie went to the drugstore to buy the ingredients in the cow ointment, then raced home to her collection of herbs. She mixed the store-bought ingredients with egg, sage, and other herbs and rubbed some on a stray cat with bald patches. When the patches began filling in with soft, shiny fur, Annie was thrilled! The cat seemed happier too.

When Lillie showed Annie her dry, red scalp, Annie gave her some of the new remedy. Would it work as well on a person as it did on a cat?

Weeks later, Lillie burst into Annie's house to show off her healthy hair. "I'm going to tell all my friends," she said. "What's it called?"

Annie thought for a moment. "Wonderful Hair Grower. That'll be 25 cents." Annie Malone, inventor, businesswoman, beauty expert, was on her way!

Over the next ten years, Annie invented more natural hair treatments. It was time to expand. She moved to Brooklyn, Illinois, a city with many Black women.

Annie loaded a horse-drawn wagon with Wonderful Hair Grower, buckets of hot water, and a chair. When she spotted groups of women leaving church and club meetings, Annie pulled up alongside and gave a short talk on proper hair care.

"No more suffering with burned scalps," she promised.
"No more hiding under big hats."

Next, Annie invited one lucky lady to come up for a free wash and style. Afterwards, Annie turned the woman around to face the crowd and let the cheers of admiration and a few "hallelujahs!" wash over her.

Bottles of Wonderful Hair Grower sold out in minutes.

In 1904, it was time to expand again, so Annie moved to St. Louis, Missouri. She added cleansing cream, shampoo, conditioner, soap, lipstick, and face powder to her line of beauty products. Sales sizzled. Annie named her company Poro, a West African word for physical and spiritual growth. She believed that if Black women improved their appearance, they'd feel better about themselves and succeed in other areas of their lives.

Most St. Louis stores were owned by whites who refused to carry the products of women of color, so Annie went door to door. Many women who tried Poro creams were so happy, they wanted to work for Annie. But before they could operate their own hair salons using the "Poro System" and selling Poro products, Annie insisted they go to school to learn all about hair and body care.

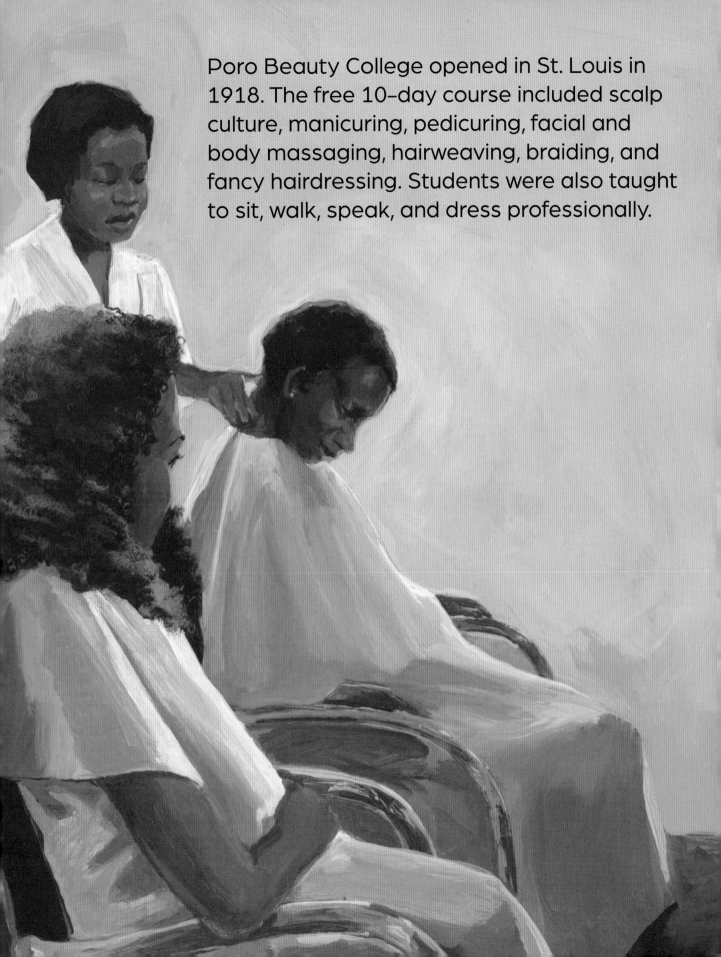

Poro Beauty College opened in St. Louis in 1918. The free 10-day course included scalp culture, manicuring, pedicuring, facial and body massaging, hairweaving, braiding, and fancy hairdressing. Students were also taught to sit, walk, speak, and dress professionally.

Poro sales agents were paid ten times what they had earned as cooks, nannies, laundresses, or maids. Annie had done what she'd promised Lillie all those many years ago — she'd turned her passion into a thriving business.

Not just for her, but for many other women. She showed them a path toward independence, pride, and dignity — along with beautiful hair.

Author's Note

After slavery ended, one way Black women celebrated their freedom was by shedding hairstyles and head coverings worn while toiling in the fields or working indoors. They didn't want reminders of those years of oppression. No more cornrows! No more scarves! They wanted the same fashionable hairstyles white women had.

Annie Minerva Turnbo Malone was an inventor and an entrepreneur, an educator and humanitarian. She helped Black women not only feel better about themselves, she helped members of this underserved community reshape and improve their lives.

Annie cared deeply about the well-being of others. Five-year employees of her company received diamond rings. Attendance and punctuality were rewarded as well. Poro College provided a place for African Americans and major Black organizations to meet since white society denied them access to public areas. When a tornado hit St. Louis in 1927, Annie let the city use Poro headquarters as a relief center, sheltering and feeding 5,000 people a day.

There were 32 Poro school branches and 75,000 Poro sales agents around the world.

Annie's legacy as a pioneer in the beauty and cosmetic industry has been overshadowed by Madam C. J. Walker, the hair-care company started and owned by Sarah Breedlove, a former employee of Annie Malone's. Breedlove modeled her products after Annie's, but didn't originate the Black beauty business and was not, as many believed, the first self-made African American female millionaire. That distinction belongs to trailblazer Annie Malone.

Annie never graduated high school because of frequent illness, but her career accomplishments earned her honorary degrees from four colleges.

By 1951, Annie was 74 and slowing down. Poro closed its doors. Annie Malone died six years later at 79.

Annie was married and divorced twice and never had children. By the time she passed away, she'd donated much of her fortune to Black causes and charities (universities, YMCAs, and orphanages).

The Annie Malone Children and Family Service Center, which Annie helped build in 1922, is still in operation in St. Louis. It began as an orphanage for Black children.

Every year, there is an Annie Malone May Day Parade in St. Louis, the oldest Black parade in the city.

Timeline

1877 – Born in Metropolis, IL, one of 10 children, to former enslaved people.

1888 – Begins braiding and styling her sisters' hair.

1898 – She and sister Laura experiment with herb- and oil-based
shampoos and "hair grower."

1900 – She and Laura move to Brooklyn, IL and sell a product they
invented called "Wonderful Hair Grower."

1902 – Moves her growing business to St. Louis, Missouri and marries Nelson
Pope (divorced 1907).

1904 – Has a store at the St. Louis World's Fair and demonstrates "Wonderful Hair
Grower" to people from all around the world.

1906 – Trademarks company name, "Poro."

1909 – Annie's sister Laura and early business partner dies of unknown causes.

1914 – Marries Aaron Malone (divorced 1924).

1918 – Opens Poro Beauty College in St. Louis (the first cosmetology school
specializing in Black hair). Eventually there are 32 Poro beauty schools
in the United States.

1926 – Poro employs 175 people in St. Louis and 75,000 beauty agents worldwide
(including the Caribbean and Africa).

1927 – After a tornado in St. Louis, Poro College becomes a rescue center that
shelters and feeds 5,000 people a day.

1930 – Poro College relocates to Chicago, IL where it takes up an entire city block.

1951 – Loses the business due to financial problems stemming from her divorce
and the stock market crash of the 1930s.

1957 – Dies of a stroke at the age of 79.

"I would be no happier than giving service to my people."
– Annie Turnbo Malone

Bibliography

Whitfield, John H. *A Friend to All Mankind: Mrs. Annie Turnbo Malone and Poro College.*
    South Carolina: CreateSpace Independent Publishing Platform, 2015.

Wilkerson, J.L. *Story of Pride, Power and Uplift: Annie T. Malone.* New York:
    Acorn Books, 2003.

Wills, Shomari. *Black Fortunes: The Story of the First Six African Americans Who Survived
    Slavery and Became Millionaires.* New York: Amistad, 2018

About the Authors

Eve Nadel Catarevas enjoys discovering little-known historical figures and sharing their achievements with others. Eve lives in Westport, CT with two- and four-legged family members.

Felicia Marshall draws on her childhood experiences in rural Texas for her illustrations. Her most recent book with Creston, *Beautiful Shades of Brown*, was an NCSS-CBC Notable Social Studies Trade Book, a Eureka Honor Book, and won the Northern Lights Book Award.